Values

How to Bring Values to Life in your Business

Ed Mayo

Greenleaf
PUBLISHING

Published by
Greenleaf Publishing Limited
Aizlewood's Mill, Nursery Street
Sheffield S3 8GG, UK
www.greenleaf-publishing.com

Printed and bound by Printondemand-worldwide.com, UK

Mixed Sources
Product group from well-managed forests, and other controlled sources
www.fsc.org Cert no. TT-COC-002641
© 1996 Forest Stewardship Council

Cover by Sadie Gornall-Jones

British Library Cataloguing in Publication Data:
A catalogue record for this book is available from the British Library.
ISBN-13: 9781783535347 [paperback]
ISBN-13: 9781783535354 [hardback]
ISBN-13: 9781783535316 [PDF ebook]
ISBN-13: 9781783535330 [ePub ebook]

Abstract

WHAT MATTERS TO US? One way of answering that question is through the lens of values, which have a powerful influence on our attitudes and behaviours. Yet it can be difficult for businesses to realise the true potential of values, which is to engage staff, customers and suppliers in an emotional way that touches on their own core motivations.

Drawing on a range of case studies worldwide, including 'profit with purpose' businesses such as co-operatives, this short guide reveals how to make a success of values. By unpacking what we mean by 'values' and 'ethics' and setting out a series of practical approaches, Ed Mayo presents how values can become a natural part of commercial life. The book identifies the pitfalls and the potential of bringing values into the heart of an organisation, from a bank that responds to an ethical crisis through to a fast-growing worker co-operative founded on the values of equality.

The values that guide your business are not necessarily the ones that are written down or that you would expect. There is no one right or wrong set of values, but there is power and potential in making the most of the values that are right for the business you are in. By reading *Values: How to Bring Values to Life in Your Business*, you will find out more about the business that you are, and the business that you could be.

About the Author

ED MAYO is a leader in the co-operative business sector. He is Secretary General at Co-operatives UK, which develops and promotes member-owned enterprises.

Ed has helped to start a wide range of businesses and social ventures, including as one of the team that started the Fairtrade Mark. He ran the award-winning ethical think-tank the New Economics Foundation for 11 years, and is the co-author of *Co-operative Advantage* (published by New Internationalist), as well as previous books on marketing, banking and micro-finance. Ed is formerly a Young Global Leader, nominated by the World Economic Forum, and has been awarded an honorary doctorate at London Metropolitan University for his work on ethical markets.

Acknowledgments

THIS SHORT BOOK started in conversation and blossomed as a result of dialogues I have been able to have with a wide range of colleagues and friends. What began as a loose and open flow of draft blog posts became, through comment and challenge, I hope a more coherent account.

I am pleased to acknowledge the debt on this text that I owe to David Aeron Thomas, Jon Alexander, Catherine Barber-Brown, Karen Bateson, Toby Blume, Iris Bohnet, Simon Burall and colleagues at Involve, Bob Cannell, Laura Carstensen, Simon Caulkin, Rhiannon Colvin, Hilary Cottam along with Katherine Garrett-Cox, Mabel van Oranje, Nicole Schwab and colleagues in the Young Global Leader community, Tom Crompton, Dave Dulson, Jon Earls, Hanan El-Youssef, Shelagh Everett, Ruth FitzJohn, Chuck Gould, Victoria Hall, Marie Harder and Firooz Firoozm and their colleagues at the Values and Sustainability Research Group at the University of Brighton, Cathryn Higgs, Peter Holbrook, Ruth Kennedy, Zena King, Tim Knowles, Dirk Lehnhoff, Martin Lowry, Josh MacAlister, Anita Mangan, Guy Mason, Nick Matthews, Agnès Mathis, Karen Miner, Nick Money, Melina Morrison, Caroline Naett, Agnes Nairn, Sonja Novkovic, Martin Parker, Michelle Parkin-Kelly, Simon Parkinson, Richard Pennycook, Courtney Plank, David Rodgers, Gianluca Salvatori and colleagues at Euricse, Richard Self, Giles Simon, Shaun Tarbuck, Stewart Wallis, Britta Werner, David Wheeler and Simon Zadek.

ACKNOWLEDGMENTS

The illustrations are by Frankie Mayo – thank you. The illustration of two heads is inspired by the work of AltGen, the London-based youth co-operative agency.

....

Contents

CHAPTER 1
What are Values?

WHAT MATTERS TO US?

One way of answering that question is through the lens of values. Our values influence both our attitudes and our behaviours. They affect how we behave in a powerful way. But they are not easy always to engage.

It is easy to pay lip service to values and many businesses do. It is harder to realise the true potential of values, which is to engage staff, customers and suppliers in an emotional way that touches on their own core motivations. Drawing on a range of case studies worldwide, including 'profit with purpose' businesses such as co-operatives, and relevant academic research, this book is a short guide to making a success of values.

My aim is to unpack for you what we mean by values and ethics and set out a series of practical approaches, with advice on bringing values to life. The values that guide your business are not necessarily the ones that are written down or that you would expect. The book explores a series of case studies, identifying the pitfalls and the potential of bringing values into the heart of an organisation, from a bank that responds to an ethical crisis through to a fast-growing worker co-operative founded on the values of equality.

Business can be a way to change the world around us, for better or worse, and, if you accept that, then values can be seen as a natural part of commercial life. Values are what motivate us. Values help us to work together. But values also challenge us. I hope that, in reading this book, you will find out more about the business that you are, and the business that you could be.

But, first, a small introduction to values as motivation in social psychology, the academic discipline that underpins so much contemporary work on values (ethics, sociology, theology and behavioural economics... we can leave those until later). This is done through the retelling of the fable of the carrot and the stick... and the rose.

Values are what motivate us

If you woke up one morning as a donkey, the choice between the carrot or the stick might be more than just a metaphor. You are stubborn, of course, and, after the metamorphosis, probably a little prickly. The carrot dangled in front of you is to encourage you to get up. For now, of course, you can think of little you'd find more tasty.

But getting up is not quite what you feel like. So, next, the stick gives you a thwack. Even with your new thick hide, it is a bit painful. The carrot and the stick seem to be opposites. But they are designed to do the same thing: to get us to behave. In the language of economics, both would be classed as 'incentives'. But, you might muse, with all the costs of carrot growing and stick wielding, isn't there a better way to influence donkeys... and people?

So, a little psychology comes to mind. Punishments and rewards for behaviour tend to be set by someone else. Both carrot and stick are externally controlled – or 'extrinsic' in terms of the motivation of the person being targeted. There is a different way. It is called the theory of self-determination, a fairly well-established and proven approach in social psychology that says that what makes us happy to act is down to what we feel from inside – 'intrinsic' motivations, such as our personal values. Acting on our intrinsic values keeps us satisfied and motivated. It saves on the costs of carrots and sticks.

We can call this the rose: an alternative motivation to both the carrot and the stick. The rose is a thing of beauty. It draws you to act because you already care for it, rather than being an instrument of pain, or gain, to induce you to change course.

WHAT MAKES US ACT ?
The Carrot and Stick ... or the Rose

and   or

EXTRINSIC   INTRINSIC
MOTIVATION   MOTIVATION

What lies behind are values. As defined by *Oxford English Dictionary*, values are 'principles or standards of behaviour; one's judgement about what is important in life.'[1]

In passing, it is worth noting that, by this definition, values are about what matters and what motivates people, whether through carrot, stick or rose, not necessarily about what is ethical or unethical. Ethical values are a narrower set – ones that make a wider normative claim about how to live or act. As eighteenth-century German philosopher Immanuel Kant saw it, values like pleasure, courage or power are not ethical because there are times when they are associated with unethical outcomes. An ethical value, such as caring or forgiveness, is something that is always good in itself, from anyone's rational perspective, and therefore has a claim on us in terms of giving us a duty to act where we can.

There can certainly be an extraordinary motive power to the roses of ethical values, as we will come to explore, but it is mistaken to think that business behaviour you might not approve of is not shaped by values. They may just be the wrong values – for example, of power, status or personal greed. To effect change, though, values are still where you have to start.

Values help us to work together

So, how do values emerge in the first place? There is a new branch of science – moral cognition – that combines social psychology with other disciplines such as studies of the brain, and suggests one answer. Shared values evolved as an effective strategy for group survival, creating a willingness to act for the benefit of others, even at a personal cost. Harvard Professor Joshua Greene puts it like this: 'We have co-operative brains because co-operation provides material benefits, biological resources that enables our genes to make copies of themselves. Out of evolutionary dirt grows the flower of human goodness.'[2]

So, the need to collaborate shapes the evolution of group values over time, but it doesn't specify what those values should be. Human values over time, including the deeper framing of faith and religion, are fabulously diverse. Football hooligans have values. The mafia has values. They're not what most would share but they offer a linked code, a 'moral syndrome' that they can coalesce around as a group. What then holds one group together may divide or conflict with another. As James Q. Wilson, author of *The Moral Sense*, comments, 'arguments about values often turn into fights about values'.[3]

Standing up for our values is part of that evolutionary imprint. We are willing to do the right thing, despite the possible costs of doing so – that is what moral theorists tend to focus on. But we are also willing to challenge those who act unfairly, despite the possible costs of doing so. Our instinctive watchful eye for free riders and cheats (or 'defectors' in the language of game theory) is one of the reasons why we watch hours of murder mysteries and detective series on TV. We are hooked not just by the plotline but for evolutionary reasons, in which our instincts are essential components of a culture encouraging values of co-operation.

Values challenge us

In business, we rely on laws, contracts and regulation to catch cheats. But you can't legislate for every eventuality. That is perhaps why regulators are moving away from detailed prescription towards 'principles-based regulation', because values might offer a more effective and more future-proof way of covering the complexity of what the licence to do business should or should not cover. Similarly, within a business, you can't set everything down in a commercial or employment agreement. Sure, you cover what you can; you fall back on the law when you have to. But values shape how people interact in a business. The best teams, the most agile businesses, move at the speed of the values they share, rather than the clauses of their contracts. They also have, by the way, a commercial advantage that is hard to steal – someone who leaves can't take the culture of shared values with them to a competitor.

When things go wrong in business, then, after the crisis, it is often to values to which managers return. Later on, as a case study, I will look at the intriguing story of a global bank, Barclays, after the crisis and scandals of the credit crunch.

Of course, it is more comfortable to do some of this in a more human-scale setting of a small business or social enterprise. It is hard for mainstream businesses to be authentic about ethical values, such as sustainability or equality, because, unlike principles of customer service or making money, they don't necessarily fit well with the reality of power and control.

Professor Gideon Kunda of Tel-Aviv University, who researches organisational culture, describes today's approach by managers to encouraging the value of teamwork in many an enterprise as a form of 'deep acting' – what he characterises as the 'feigned solidarity' of the modern workplace.[4] Finton O'Toole, writing in the *Irish Times*, talks of the toxic effect that high pay and bonuses for leaders can have on their workforce. Many low-paid jobs are demanding, but there can be a dignity to work: 'most people actually want to do their jobs well and do them honourably'.[5] If business leaders equate status with pay, it is hard to demonstrate that they believe in the dignity of their workforce.

So values are not easy. But that is because values challenge us. They ask hard questions. Above all, what are you in business for? All businesses are there for a purpose and, to be truly coherent, their values should not just illustrate how to achieve that purpose but also exclude practices that get in the way.

If we took ethical values in business as seriously as we take their inventory and finance, we could see very different patterns of business and business leadership emerge over time.

CHAPTER 2

Organising Values

BEFORE WE COME TO WIDER BUSINESS, a good place to start, if we are to explore values in the life of organisations, is with values-rich voluntary initiatives. One academic who researches this is Professor Marie Harder of Fudan University in China. Over the last few years, Marie and her team have worked with a series of community organisations to look at their values in practice.

In any organisation, people involved may share values and have their own distinctive personal values. There may then be different partners, with different interests and values. As a result, what is important overall may be difficult to assess – and when it comes to evaluating community projects, the tendency is to reflect the values of the funders or simply what can easily be measured.

Marie has developed a process for identifying and mapping the values that matter. Her method is one of eliciting values, by rooting them in an open and deliberative process based on context and behaviours. Her work with the European urban design agency The Glass-House, for example, helped them to surface four different circles of values:

- Values that are not shared,

- Values that are contested,

- Values that are shared and important to us, and then

- The core values that are central to who we are.

The exercise of mapping the different values, says The Glass-House Chief Executive Sophia de Sousa, gave her team confidence to engage people in a different way: 'at the beginning we were very much a community support organisation. People now see us as an organisation rooted in very clear principles and values.'[6]

In Mexico, Marie and fellow academics from the Values and Sustainability Research Group at the University of Brighton worked with a children's environmental charity, the Echeri Children's Group. To elicit values, they used a game that the children knew and liked, which was to paint on each other's hands. They were asked to paint how they felt at the end of activities like planting trees – and then describe what they had painted.

Alongside being happy or tired, they then used words such as pride and wonder. Values such as these are usually neglected in project evaluations because they are seen as intangible and tough to measure. What the exercise helped the Echeri Children's Group to build was a new, more realistic but also more magical account of their efforts. An organisation that used to track its success by counting the number of trees planted and the number of children involved now also reports on the emotional connection of the children with nature and the sense of equality across those involved.

In search of coherence

When it comes to values in business, I have learned more from my former colleague at the New Economics Foundation Simon Zadek than from any other. Simon and I won support from the Paul Hamlyn Foundation for a research programme he ran called Values Based Organisation – an alternative to the dominant business frameworks of the time focused on structure and strategy. The initiative gave birth to modern social accounting.

The UK fair trade company Traidcraft was founded in 1979 (solving the recycled toilet paper needs of my mother and father for the following two decades). By 1992 the owners, the trustees of Traidcraft Foundation, were wondering how the organisation was doing. They knew exactly what the sales were, what the product range was, who the customers were, but they didn't know how they were performing against their values – which were, in short, love and justice in world trade. We worked with Traidcraft on a model of social audit that Simon developed, which answered the question by asking the right people – the stakeholders of the company, who could both reflect on Traidcraft's values and assert perspectives based on their own.

For example, Traidcraft suppliers, producer co-ops in countries such as the Philippines, Kenya and Tanzania, put more emphasis on the longer-term relationship with the business, including better-quality and more timely information on market trends, rather than the sales volumes that were previously assumed to be their concern. Fair trade for them was about market information and product development, as much as about price and margin.

One of the results of the early social audits was a re-articulation of Traidcraft's values. Out went love and justice in world trade, although the spirit of that remained, and in came something more focused – to fight poverty through trade, practising and promoting approaches to trade that help poor people in developing countries transform their lives.

A second organisation we worked with was one in which that greater edge and practicality of purpose, rather than reinforcing core values, risked being at odds with them. Sarvodaya Shramadana Movement is one of the largest development agencies in Asia. Founded on Buddhist principles by the inspiring figure, Dr A.T. Ariyaratne, Sarvodaya today supports self-help in around 15,000 villages in Sri Lanka. But while its values were rooted in self-help, by the 1990s the organisation at national level had become a conduit for development assistance from overseas. Our work with them suggested that this brought with it a subtle shift of values, however unintentional. The framework of reporting on aid, for example, put the perspective of outside funders ahead of the villages to which the central body was supposed to be accountable. They had more money coming in, but were, it seemed, less responsive, less effective in harnessing self-help than before.

All values, Simon stresses, need to be renewed over time – being part of an organisation's past doesn't necessarily make them part of its future. You can have values as part of your founding story, but if they don't resonate anymore, they become archaic. It is therefore a common pitfall to romanticise values in organisations.

The key is to see how values help connect. What makes an institution effective is not any particular set of values, rules or structures, but the level of 'organisational coherence' they offer in practice. Where values are shared and support a coherent, aligned approach across those involved in the business, there is a natural teamwork and co-production that becomes the default. Where values are not shared and pull activity in different, incoherent directions, the result is confusion.

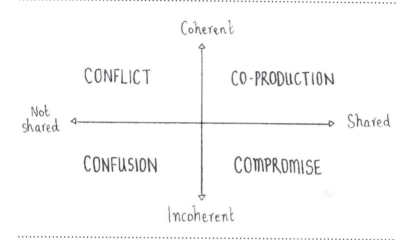

Coherent

CONFLICT | CO-PRODUCTION

Not shared ← → Shared

CONFUSION | COMPROMISE

Incoherent

Chiming with the wider social, economic and political environment is part of this story. Values are in their nature contextual, Simon explains. Different values can express themselves in very different organisational forms. Which values have the greatest resonance will vary across time, place and context. Automobiles were first developed for the elite in aristocratic Europe, all hand-crafted. It took a different set of values, in America, to manufacture them for the masses. I call this 'the values fit'. We will come later to a case study of Nokia, which in an earlier life produced car tyres (today, mobile telephony) and chose values but failed to find a fit.

At the other end of the spectrum from coherence is 'organisational neurosis': a fragmentation of direction, effort and commitment, with a knock-on loss of effectiveness. In the business world, it is typically where the interests or values of staff, customers or suppliers collide with those of the owners.

All organisations have to chime with the world around them. Values are a key part of that story.

....

CHAPTER 3

How do Values Play Out in Business?

HISTORICALLY, QUAKER AND NON-CONFORMIST COMPANIES in England were famed for their ethics. Barclays Bank came from that tradition.

In 2012, the values of Barclays hit a new low, when, with a number of other global banks, it was fined for its role in manipulating the LIBOR interest rate, a reference for credit right across the market. The bank had demonstrated, in the words of its chairman, unacceptable standards of behaviour. The chief executive resigned and the bank appointed Antony Jenkins as a new CEO, to clean up the stables – and focus on values.

Jenkins in turn commissioned an eight-month independent investigation, the Salz Review, at a cost of US$21 million to report on how to change the values that had led the organisation astray. In the same chapter of thinking as critiques of 'institutional racism' (a phrase coined by the black power activist and pioneer Stokely Carmichael), organisational values were in the dock.

Salz concluded that 'Barclays should set clear targets against which to assess progress on embedding the values necessary to build a strong ethical culture. Progress against these targets should be measured through employee, customer and other stakeholder surveys and should be reported regularly.'[7] Barclays then set about implementing the report, with a programme to manage staff performance against a set of core values, including integrity and respect for others.

But changing values and culture takes time. Jenkins was appointed as chief executive to clean up the bank and within three years the board had changed its mind. What they wanted was to boost earnings. The new executive chairman, John McFarlane, explained that Jenkins 'was good at executing what we asked him to do at that time. What we are asking him to do now is different.'[8]

Of course, values are not just about leaders, as we will look at later on, but you wouldn't now get good odds on the chances of long-term success for the programme on values at Barclays. In 2015, Barclays was one of six global banks fined US$5.6 billion for rigging the foreign exchange markets. Foreign exchange traders had used chatrooms, with names such as 'The Cartel' to influence the value of major currencies. 'If you ain't cheating, you ain't trying' was the comment of one Barclays' trader in a chatroom.[9] The bank had resisted a settlement that other banks had agreed with the US competition authorities and fought it to the end.

Barclays is a curious case of how to set about changing values... and then fail. It is a reminder of the saying that businesses don't have a culture – they are a culture. But the lessons of the Salz Review also go deeper according to one person who submitted evidence to it: Douglas Board. The terms of review compromised the exercise, he argues, because they were based on the illusion of control.

The aim was to identify weaknesses in values and set them right, with stronger assurance methods to address deviation in future. This was as if Barclays was a home with a central heating thermostat that the

Bank could control, adjusting as needed. But values don't work like that. With the scale and complexity of the bank, control by those in charge was not likely to succeed if it wasn't matched by the development of a constituency for change across the bank and the capabilities to sustain a more appropriate set of values. The Salz Review, says Douglas Board, was 'giving the Bank ethical fish with varying (but not indefinite) sell-by dates, not teaching the Bank to fish ethically.'[10]

Leadership on values, it turns out, is about facilitation, not instruction.

One in four new entrepreneurs are values-driven

What about businesses at the other end of the scale? Do many kitchen-table enterprises and small businesses count on values?

Rebecca Harding is an entrepreneur who is an authority on entrepreneurship. In the early 2000s, she co-designed the Global Entrepreneurship Monitor. Then, in 2012, running her own business, she set out to explore the motivations of people like her, interviewing 2,500 entrepreneurs across 13 countries.

The people she surveyed were running businesses that were older than two years but younger than ten. They had already achieved turnovers of US$300,000 or above (or national equivalent) and so were set on a 'growth path'. Rebecca set out to discover what their values and motivations were for setting up in business. I helped her to publish the results.[11]

What she found was that one of the most common reasons for starting a business, cited by 47% of entrepreneurs from all countries, is 'making a difference'. This includes factors such as social benefits, environmental improvement and creating jobs. Of these who cite 'making a difference' as one of their values, close to 43% say that it is their primary motivation. Where it is a primary motive, which is one in four overall, we can call these entrepreneurs 'values-driven'. Where it is a secondary motive, 'values-aware'.

Respondents in Germany and South Africa emerge as the most collaborative in terms of motivation to make a difference. Three out of five (60%) of growth-oriented entrepreneurs in Germany are primarily motivated to start up in business in order to make a difference ('values-driven'). 84% of entrepreneurs in Germany say that this is a motivation, whether primary or not ('values-aware').

Rather than this being a trade-off, there is higher perceived business performance among values-driven entrepreneurs: they emerge as more innovative as enterprises than those businesses who do not have 'making a difference' as their primary aim. This holds too in emphatic fashion for entrepreneurs surveyed in the 'BRICSA' nations of Brazil, Russia, India, China and South Africa.

The idea of 'profit with purpose', of a collaborative mindset, is miles away from the myth of the heroic loner, the John Wayne model of entrepreneur that is glorified by TV programmes such as *The Apprentice*. It is true for some. But to strip out values and elevate the story of the self-oriented lone entrepreneur into the only way to see entrepreneurship is an act of economic self-harm. The picture of the real values and motivation of entrepreneurs that Rebecca Harding paints is complex, rather than simple, and social as much as financial.

So, here is the potential: if we can offer a better balance, with a recognition of the role of values in business, then we can start to harness the true power of entrepreneurship, to improve the world around us.

But to do that there is an important qualification to make: that there is often a difference between what your starting motivation is and what your final behaviour turns out to be. This is the values–action gap.

Not all values lead to action

In 1988, John Elkington and Julia Hailes launched the first great modern wave of interest in ethical consumers, with their practical handbook *The Green Consumer Guide*. It sold a million copies worldwide.

It ought to have changed the world but, so far, it hasn't. The reason is what researchers have dubbed a values–action gap. As a rule of thumb, what people do with their ethical values is around one-tenth of what they say they would like to do, in the reflective context of a focus group or market research survey: 30% intention versus 3% action on ethical values. The primary factor is habit, and a degree of inertia. Making conscious choices is harder work and, most of the time, we fall back on routines that keep things simple.

The same values–action gap holds for business. There are plenty of values listed by large companies. But little has changed since the *Harvard Business Review* in 2002 exposed a widespread 'debasement' of values in business – concluding that while 80% of large companies worldwide 'tout their values publicly', these are values like ambition, speed or excellence that 'too often stand for nothing but a desire to be au courant or, worse still, politically correct.'[12]

In the UK, 90% of top companies have a clear statement of values and expected behaviours, but research suggests that few if any track or report on how they live up to them. 'Integrity' is the most cited value, followed by 'passion'. Around one in four companies claim that passion is a core value, but there is no evidence that staff or customers feel the love.[13] Passion, too, is one value that has been hollowed out by over-use over time – its origins, after all, are in the passion, or suffering, of Jesus Christ on the cross.

Values that matter

Tom Crompton has worked on environmental causes for many years, and now runs an initiative, Common Cause, designed to reboot the way that business and NGOs approach values.

In line with the framework of carrots, sticks and roses described earlier, Tom draws a distinction between 'intrinsic' values, which are inner-directed

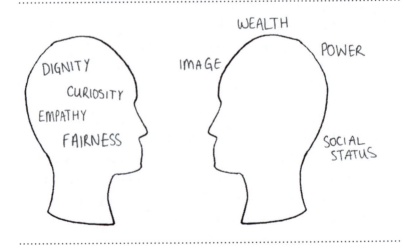

and more personal, and 'extrinsic' values such as outer-directed concerns about wealth, social status or image. Intrinsic values do tend to favour co-operation, with motives such as fairness and sustainability, while extrinsic values are more influenced by competition, such as financial gain or personal advantage.

There are good reasons, he says, why it is important to understand which of these sets of values are being prompted. First, if you talk to people in the language of extrinsic values, with marketing such as 'pay less', 'get ahead' or 'be cool', you tend to anaesthetise their intrinsic values. He points to a slew of studies, for example, in which 'participants who are temporarily more aware of money, image or status show lower levels of social and environmental concern'.

Second, if you engage people by prompting one of their intrinsic values, such as fairness, they are more likely to respond in relation to other similar values as well. 'There is good empirical evidence that these "bleed over" between one another,' explains Tom. 'Engage one and you are likely to strengthen others. This is why we find that we can talk to people about "supporting self-direction among people with disabilities", and see an upturn in environmental concern.'[14]

What this means is that it doesn't matter too much which of these intrinsic values you are working on. In pursuing one you are likely to be strengthening them all.

Of course, plenty of businesses are successful with an appeal to power and social status. Plenty of businesses operate with values that are unstated and unarticulated, but still powerful enough to prompt corporate behaviours that are far from ethical. Focusing primarily on intrinsic values is a different approach to business and offers a different profile of business benefits.

So, what social entrepreneurs and ethical businesses can do is to understand which intrinsic values are likely to 'bleed over' and strengthen others that matter – to develop a 'palette' of shared values supportive of genuine sustainability or social change.

The business case for shared values

So, what is the business case for shared values?[15]

First, it is worth remembering that there is plenty of evidence that businesses with strong sets of values perform better than those without. Research on around 700 firms, using five years of data compiled by the Great Place to Work initiative, suggests that, while there is no performance link with firms that have simply published a set of values, there is a strong positive link with those firms whose values are seen within the company to be prominent.[16]

VALUES ARE LIKE A

NORTHBOUND TRAIN

At their best, shared values create a northbound train – the effect of everybody focused on the same direction. At their worst, a clash of values can distract and destroy any business.

What the research can't prove, though, is whether this is correlation or causation. Is it the case that the best-performing firms are so well organised that, as an illustration of their high performance, they have strong, embedded values? Or is it the case that those values help to reinforce and even drive that high performance?

As an interesting aside, the same research concludes that going public reduces the extent to which companies can focus on 'integrity as short-term decisions can carry undue weight. Privately-owned companies (including venture capital-backed organisations) tend to have higher levels of integrity than publicly-quoted companies.'[17] As we will explore in the next chapter, in the story of co-operative enterprises worldwide, there can be a powerful alignment between the 'hard side' of business structure and ownership, and the 'soft side' of business values and culture.

A different way to approach the case for investing in intrinsic values is the extent to which they can drive positive norms and behaviours, such as loyalty or ideas for innovation, in customers, suppliers or employees. The extraordinary success of open source or free software, the importance of volunteering in civil society, the power and reach of faith communities, are examples of institutional activity that are dependent on the free and willing collaboration of people on the basis of sufficient overlap of values and purpose.

In commercial business, where participation is subject to contract and compensation, there are times when that same voluntarism, or 'discretionary effort' in the jargon, is critical to the enterprise. One example is staff retention. For larger firms, staff recruitment is one of the clearest cost variables – and, if having values that they care about in the workplace can encourage more staff to stay, the financial gains are significant.

One estimate is that the total cost of replacing an outgoing member of staff is US$43,000 – or US$29,000 in retail, where staff turnover rates can be as high as 40% each year. Mostly these are hidden costs in lost productivity. But stripping down the numbers and just looking at advertising, backfill, interviewing and administration, the costs come to more than US$7,000 on average.[18] In short, for any 1% turnover reduced through an investment in values, the business benefits add up to significant sums.

The effect of values on business performance is explored in the academic research around employee ownership. Research by the Cass Business School shows that giving employees an ownership stake in the business significantly boosts their productivity.[19]

In a 2016 report, Professor Virginie Pérotin draws on a range of international econometric studies to conclude that businesses create more sustainable employment where they are structured as worker co-operatives, in which the key feature is active employee control of, and involvement in, the life of the firm rather than philanthropic ownership in the name of employees. Studies of family-owned firms likewise argue for an approach to ownership that includes its psychological dimension – the *feeling* of ownership – as crucial for understanding family business in addition to formal, legal ownership structures.[20] Here is the magic of pride as a value, once again.

So there is a business case for values, but let's turn that on its head. What happens if being unethical is even better for sales?

A survey in 2012 of 500 financial services professionals in the US and the UK suggested that one in four believe that, in order to succeed, financial services professionals may need to engage in unethical or illegal conduct. A similar number reported that they have first-hand knowledge of wrongdoing in their workplace.[21] To be ethical in a market that is systemically unethical is a point of differentiation, but may also be a straight commercial cost or risk.

Does that mean that the business case fails? Well, not necessarily. We are conditioned to accept too narrow a view of what business is and can be; there is always a larger story than money. It all depends on your values. At root, the business case for ethical values such as fairness or sustainability is for the sake of fairness or sustainability.

....

CHAPTER 4

Co-operatives as a Test-case of Values in Action

SUMA WAS FOUNDED AS A BUSINESS IN 1975 and moved to its current purpose-built distribution centre in Yorkshire, England, in 2001. It is the market leader in wholefood distribution, distributing 7,000 vegetarian product lines across the UK including several hundred own-brand products.

Last year, Suma delivered its best trading performance for 35 years, turning over US$49 million. Equality is one of its values as a co-operative and as such this means operating on the basis of equal pay.

This is not for everyone, and it is vital for the business that those who come to work and become members are aligned with the values of equality and prepared to champion them. It translates the values into a set of five behaviours Suma is looking for.

Suma recruits all year around, through local media and invites speculative applications. Colleagues then screen them for evidence of the behaviours, hold work trials and group interviews. If successful, this then leads on to three months' probation in manual work, before six months' membership training. If you make it through that, there is then a ballot of all the members on whether you join.

The only job description it uses is that of a membership job description. Bob Cannell of Suma comments that 'we don't recruit "me too" co-operators or for vocational skills primarily. It is easier to teach a member to be an accountant than teach an accountant to be a member. We recruit for values and train for skills. Suma has used this method since the 1990s and has recruited 100 great worker co-op members by it.'[22]

It is easier to build values that flourish in the workplace, as has Suma, when it is those people that own the business. 'Working here is meaningful – whether I'm sweeping the floor or taking part in business decisions. Does being a part owner make a difference? Of course it does.' says Joe Haydn, worker-owner of Unicorn Grocery Co-op, a fast-growing worker-owned wholefood retailer in Manchester.[23]

And, once you have experienced that voice and those values, you won't want to let them go. As Debbie Harley, worker-owner of Delta T Devices, a worker-owned co-op manufacturer developing market-leading instruments for environmental science research, comments: 'I can't see myself working anywhere else where I couldn't be part of the decision process.'[24]

A global set of values

Co-operative enterprises stand out as an enduring model of business based on the idea of sharing. But they are also an interesting test-case of whether values make a difference. There is an agreed code of business values that is intended to connect and inform the behaviour of co-operative enterprises around the world. They are built into international guidelines and, in many countries, into national law.

These are the co-operative and ethical values set out by the International Co-operative Alliance in its *Statement of Co-operative Identity*.

The evolution of the values is in itself a fascinating example of deliberation within a social movement. The list emerged from an extensive global dialogue, involving consideration of values at around 10,000 meetings in different settings across the world. Sven Åke Böök reported on these in Tokyo in 1992 and they were debated by the representative Congress of the International Co-operative Alliance.

Perhaps not surprisingly, the findings were too complex to be able to digest, so the mandate was given to a working group led by Canadian Professor Ian MacPherson to develop a distilled version, of principles and values, that could apply worldwide. The *Statement of Co-operative Identity* was agreed in Manchester in 1995.

As codified by the International Co-operative Alliance, there are ten values in all – six co-operative values and four ethical values.

The co-operative values – self-help, self-responsibility, democracy, equality, equity, solidarity – describe the design of the business. The ethical values – honesty, openness, social responsibility, caring for others – describe the operation of the business. Alongside these are seven principles – three on how co-operative ownership should be structured (such as ensuring that ownership is for those that participate in the business, rather than more distant investors), three on co-operative culture (such as a commitment to education) and one on the independence of the business as a democratic enterprise. Principles, it is worth adding, are in effect values in action – a way to direct behaviour.

This list of values, as MacPherson reported,

> **"does not induce tidy uniformity...the application of 'honesty'
> can vary across different cultures and kinds of co-operatives.
> Openness depends as much on social relations within a given
> society and the management culture of a given co-operative as
> it does on generally accepted accounting standards. The point
> is that values, while they can have some similar characteristics
> around the world, also vary greatly in kinds of understanding and
> ways of being expressed.**"[25]

They are also not prescriptive, but guides for action – seen as open-ended, therefore allowing for a deepening of practice over time. Even with a single statement of values, the co-operative identity therefore has multiple personalities.

Ian MacPherson, who died in 2013, believed that values can serve a bridge between the world you live in and the world you would like to live in. 'One can never expect to achieve perfection,' he explained. 'The ideal will always be beyond one's grasp and that is partly what creates the special kind of entrepreneurship one can identify with co-operatives.'[26]

Do co-operatives use their values?

We know that co-operatives come in all shapes and sizes, and this also holds true for what they do in terms of values. The research centre EURICSE interviewed opinion leaders in the sector in 2013. They commented that, while co-ops worldwide tend to be strict on their structure, they are looser in terms of their culture. Many fail to fulfil at least one of the seven co-operative principles – the least complied with being the commitment to education, training and information.[27] In late 2015, the International Co-operative Alliance issued guidance to the principles that talks to that variability, as well as pointing to best practice. Neither initiative, however, focused on the specific use by co-operatives of the global co-operative and ethical values. So, to explore this, I worked with colleagues to research two dozen co-operatives worldwide.

Every co-op we sampled does communicate values of some kind. The global value that is most commonly promoted is 'social responsibility', followed by reference to democracy and then openness. The least cited of the global values were self-help, solidarity and caring for others.

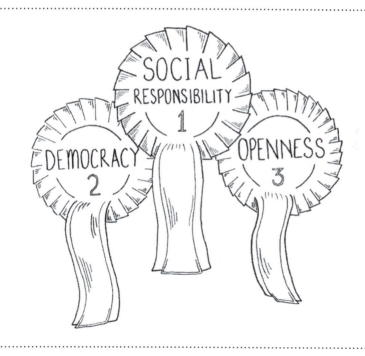

Other values cited included 'respect' and 'business longevity', with reference to ensuring business and employee relationships are strong and stable. For agricultural co-operatives this often included reference to food safety and conforming to or exceeding animal welfare requirements. 'Diversity' was also commonly referred to, and, more specifically, the commitment to 'living wages' for all employee-workers (The Hub Bicycle Co-operative, USA) and ensuring safe working conditions (Namoi Cotton, Australian agricultural co-operative).

The Spanish worker co-operative Mondragon draws on its values to extend the core list of co-operative principles from seven to ten. An example of its difference in action is on pay, as one of the first international companies to operate a ratio, set between top and bottom pay. The original ratio was up to 1:6 and was chosen as a way of encouraging managers to raise pay if they needed a pay rise themselves. In the 1980s, the ratio grew to 1:15 – as too many managers were being lured away by higher pay elsewhere. Alongside this, pay at Mondragon is set according to measures that include productivity and absenteeism and measures of how well staff members get on with other people (constituting 20% of the pay decision).[28]

Even if they come from a global statement, values have to be owned at the level of the firm, and the principle of education of members and the workforce, although not universal, is a reflection of this – that there is a need for and benefit to work to build a culture around the values of co-operation. Some, such as The Co-operative Bank in the UK (investor-owned but with co-operative values written into its articles of association) use both internal training and an interpretive framework as a result, to translate the long list of global values into a workable shorthand for the business.

The impact of the co-operative sector having a global set of values is hard to test. As Professor David Wheeler, President and Vice Chancellor of Cape Breton University, Canada, warns me: 'don't look to a static list of stated principles, when what really matters is the development, articulation and evolutionary processes that surround them.'[29] But there is some evidence to suggest that, at the very least, businesses with distinctive values may act in distinctive ways. The global values offer a prompt, or default, for co-operatives that can then be a reference point for its members. In France, co-ops are now required to conduct an independent audit for members at least once every five years to assess their co-operative difference.

In many countries, ethical values are core to the brand values of co-ops. The UK consumer research magazine *Ethical Consumer*, drawing on an extensive database of ethical screening, states that co-operative businesses are in the top third of ethical performers in 80% of the markets that they surveyed, and are the top performers in 23% of markets.[30]

The use of values in co-operatives is mixed and varied, certainly not always well understood, but is encouraging of the idea that values in business can indeed change the way that business is done.

CHAPTER 5

Values and Purpose

HERE IS NELSON MANDELA, in his momentous speech from the dock during the Rivonia trial:

> **"**During my lifetime I have dedicated myself to this struggle of the African people. I have fought against white domination, and I have fought against black domination. I have cherished the ideal of a democratic and free society in which all persons live together in harmony and with equal opportunities. It is an ideal which I hope to live for and to achieve. But, if needs be, it is an ideal for which I am prepared to die.**"**

He names four values that he holds: democracy, freedom, harmony and equality.

The text is used as a prompt by Victoria Hall, a business coach and occupational psychologist with Talent Futures, which works across 45 countries.[31] She encourages people to start with their own values, selecting these from a long list, or, for the more reflective, drawing these out of times that felt most significant or meaningful in your life. What was it that inspired you to act in the way that you did? For some, values may be bound up in an integrated philosophy, or spiritual faith – a purpose in life. Can this be shared across organisations? Can enterprises have a purpose?

Starting with purpose

In my experience, you can trace most of the lived values of an organisation back to its founding, and its founders, however far back that may be. The start-up phase for a business can be like a forge for values, defining the organisation as it makes its own story. Airbnb global head of community Douglas Atkin sees values as critical in helping people feel like they 'belong and believe'. In 2004, he wrote *The Culting of Brands*, a book on why the best brands are like cults, with followers who are believers. These businesses are causes.

Beyond the start-up phase, and the uncertain life of cults, founding stories can also help long-established business to articulate their purpose. I am not talking about how Jack met Jill and established Long Haul Enterprises because they were wildly enthusiastic about new models of distance logistics with money from an uncle and the bank, which is often the story you get. The real stories are ones that illustrate the character of the founders, and how they have stamped this on the business.

The founder of IKEA, Ingvar Feodor Kamprad, for example, was born in March 1926 on a small farm called Elmtaryd near the village of Agunnaryd in Sweden. He began his career at the age of six, selling matches. By the age of ten, he was on a bicycle selling Christmas decorations, fish and pencils doorstep to doorstep. At the age of 17, in 1943, Kamprad's father rewarded him with a small sum of money for doing well in school, despite being dyslexic. With it he founded a business named IKEA, an abbreviation for Ingvar Kamprad from Elmtaryd, Agunnaryd, his boyhood home.[32] His were humble beginnings. It was tough times, when Sweden was agrarian and poor, evoking values of hard work, frugality and egalitarianism – values that echo in the ethos of IKEA today.

Google sets out its timeline, as well as a statement of 'ten things we know to be true', which link its back-story to its values and current perspectives on the right way to do business. Facebook, meanwhile, took a while to accept that many of its early team came from a hacker ethic. It wasn't a word that seemed very corporate to a grown-up company. In 2011, though, the street leading into Facebook HQ was named Hacker Way and the centre of its campus is Hacker Square. That doesn't make Facebook a force for freedom, but it hints perhaps of new possibilities.

Corporate culture is about shared meanings and an overlapping sense of identity. It is kept alive by stories such as founding myths, as well as by the legends of past heroes and villains. Every business is a Charles Dickens book, a story full of character, colour and complexity, even if every business leader tends to see it as a Spielberg movie: soft-focus, touching and hopeful.

Also, not every movie wins favour. Hewlett Packard is good at telling the story of the original HP garage, which it describes as the 'birthplace of Silicon Valley' – although arguably the values of collaboration that Dave Packard set out with Bill Hewlett have been scarce in the conflicts and disputes of the company's recent, more troubled years. Volkswagen has a long brand legacy, but it was exactly those legacy values that were subverted from 2009 when the company engaged in profit-seeking test fixing for diesel car emissions.

Enron, the US energy and commodities giant, went bust in 2001 in a scandal of financial misreporting that then laid low their auditors, Arthur Andersen. Enron suffered from deep-seated issues of dishonesty that contaminated the organisation. But, famously, the company had operated a 64-page booklet, *The Enron Code of Ethics*. One of its values on paper was integrity – 'we work with customers and prospects openly, honestly and sincerely.'[33]

Purpose provides a rationale for why people should act and what shared values are needed to shape how they act. The emphasis on having a purpose is a welcome rebalancing from the days of narrow shareholder value, but only if the values that are claimed in that purpose or corporate story are then lived out in practice. And the warning is that sitting on a high horse means there is a long way down.

....

CHAPTER 6

Getting Going on Values

THERE IS A WORLD OF DIFFERENCE between values on paper and values in the rough and tumble of the workplace and market. But when it comes to understanding values and making them come alive, there is not a lot of guidance out there: cloud forests of books on business value, very few on business values. Values are, for example, sidelined in many business excellence models, such as the European Foundation for Quality Management. Where values do pop up is in the context of leadership. That makes sense. People may have to do what you say as a business leader, because it is visible, but they don't have to believe in what you stand for. Status alone does not cut it.

Personal values

Bill George is the former Chairman and CEO of Medtronic, the world's leading medical technology company. Now a lecturer at Harvard, and author of the book *Authentic Leadership*, he cautions that 'you do not know what your true values are until they are tested under pressure. It is relatively easy to list your values and to live by them when things are going well. It is under pressure – when your success, your career, or your life hangs in the balance – that you must decide what your values are.'[34]

'Those who develop a clear sense of their values before they get into a crisis,' he adds 'are better prepared to keep their bearings and navigate through difficult decisions and dilemmas when the pressure mounts.'[35] It helps therefore to be self-reflective. To be a leader when it comes to values is not just to champion good practice in the organisation, but also to act in person as enough of a role model. The best advice for those who want to lead on values, from Bill George, and from many other leadership guides and gurus, is therefore to be natural, be authentic, be yourself.

If it helps, one way to understand your own values, mentioned in the last chapter, is to pick out three to five from a long list of 'core values'; and I include a sample one here. Core values are the guiding concepts that shape our intentions and actions. Think of a time perhaps at which you were at your best – what motivated you? Or ask a friend – as Yale psychologist Nina Strohminger explains, 'studies show is that morality is essential to how others see you, and how they construct your identity.'[36]

For myself, one of my core values is mutuality. I owe a lot to my family and upbringing, but on this I was a rebel. The family motto was 'life isn't fair' and that was something, as a third child, I found hard to take. As a student, at a time of Live Aid and famine in Africa, I set about a range of small, collaborative social enterprises, from a fundraising book to the charity rag, to make a difference. After university, I had the privilege to be part of the team that started the international Fairtrade Mark, before working in the co-operative business sector. I accept that life isn't fair. I just want to be part of changing that.

LONG LIST OF CORE VALUES		
Acceptance	Faith	Play
Accountability	Fame	Pleasure
Adventure	Family	Politeness
Ambition	Forgiveness	Pride
Artistry	Freedom	Privacy
Authority	Friendship	Professionalism
Beauty	Fun	Quality
Caring for others	Health	Reputation
Collaboration	Honesty	Respect for tradition
Commitment	Honouring of elders	Self-help
Conformity	Humility	Self-responsibility
Control	Humour	Sense of belonging
Courage	Independence	Service
Craftsmanship	Inner harmony	Sex
Creativity	Innovation	Social power
Curiosity	Integrity	Social responsibility
Customer focus	Kindness	Solidarity
Daring	Leadership	Spirituality
Democracy	Learning	Sports
Dignity	Loyalty	Success
Empathy	Mutuality	Sustainability
Enlightenment	Nature	Teaching
Entertainment	Obedience	Teamwork
Equality	Objectivity	Tradition
Equity	Openness	Understanding
Excellence	Originality	Variety
Expertise	Passion	Wealth
Fairness	People	Wisdom

Shared values

One of the most common but understated of this list of personal values is conformity; and it is this that helps to give shared values real traction. Shared values are the motivations, explicit or implicit, that can be considered to be part of the culture of an organisation as a whole. If your business values learning, it is not that everyone has to own that as a personal value, just that enough do to make it a social norm that others will act on. There will always be sub-cultures of course in organisations – you want the professional values of accountants, not the public relations team, when it comes to signing off the accounts as true and fair. But as a leader, it is essential to bend over backwards to avoid acting in ways that undermine organisation-wide shared values. The little things done wrong fast become legends, and although you may stay in your job for years, your leadership overall is tainted from that moment.

Even in a context of change – or so-called transformational leadership – the chances of success are better if you start with an understanding of organisational culture, including its tacit rules and unwritten values. Rather than jump to assert new values which then conflict, listen, recognise and then help to articulate and adapt the best of what is already there. You don't want values to be a source of resistance to change.

You can use business anthropologists, to listen at scale, or there are useful diagnostic surveys to help, such as the Organizational Culture Assessment Instrument, Values Modes, which helps to identify common categories around shared values, or the Cultural Transformation Toolkit developed by Richard Barrett, which is framed as a journey towards a culture of consciousness. The framework on values that is widely used by researchers is that of Professor Shalom Schwartz. This is a wheel (or circumplex, for the research-minded) that turns between headings of self-enhancement (such as power, achievement and hedonism), openness to change (such as stimulation and self-direction), self-transcendence (such as universalism and benevolence) and conservation (such as security and conformity/tradition). The values wheel has been used extensively in peer-reviewed studies, which gives it strong academic weighting, and one finding is that, whatever culture they are drawn from, social groups as a whole tend ultimately to gravitate towards a common hierarchy of value priorities.

The critique of any tool such as the values wheel is that it becomes perhaps a framework that simply illuminates its own underlying assumptions. More, what it offers is not necessarily something that is easily comprehended by or comprehensible to most of the people who are the subject of it. So, the alternative, or complement, to top-down or side-in on values is to go bottom-up: to elicit values that matter by engaging with people, rather than just surfacing them through questionnaires and consultants.

A participative approach to selecting values

A bottom-up approach developed by Professor Marie Harder is one that looks to engage people in a conversation about what really matters. It aims to use values as a tool for organisational transformation. Hers is a facilitated process, and there is no guarantee that if you change the facilitator or adapt the process, you get the same results, but my experience is that the key steps are relevant to any organisation looking to articulate its values:

1. Start by exploring what the business means to those who are involved with it, so that work in values is rooted in the context of

the wider organisation. That may mean telling stories or perhaps picking out pictures from magazines that bring the organisation as a whole to life.

2. If you are engaging a wider set of people in identifying values, then separate out different stakeholder groups, so that there is an allowance for the way that a difference of interests can equal a difference of perspective on values. If you are just working with staff, then don't lose sight of what other groups, suppliers, customers, the ultimate owners may consider to be of value.

3. Don't start with high-level and highfalutin values. Start instead with a long list of more concrete 'values guides' – which are statements of how people may behave in line with specific values. I give a sample set here of these I have used for co-operative enterprises. Ask in groups which of these is most reflective and most important to the organisation, inside and out. Knock them about, change the words, add to them, split them and, above all, get them into a list, whether ten or twenty, that comprise a good start.

4. From these, you can then start to draw out the higher values that matter most, again choosing your words in ways that fit and that talk to those involved rather than sticking to pre-set formulas.

5. Test the results against step 1, where you started, and adapt and repeat as needed.

VALUES GUIDES FOR CO-OPERATIVES

CORE VALUES	VALUES IN ACTION. PEOPLE...
Self-help	...are encouraged to reach their potential
	...have self-respect
	...express their opinions openly and honestly
	...make suggestions for ways to improve the business
Self-responsibility	...are encouraged or supported to fulfil their responsibilities
	...are motivated and productive in their work
	...put things into practice, where there is shared agreement to act in a certain way
	...understand the framework of values, principles and rules that govern the organisation
Democracy	...take part in decisions that affect them directly
	...have an equal opportunity to express their opinions
	...have a sense of power that they can help make change happen
	...are engaged in strategic planning
Equality	...respect the opinions of others
	...have an equal opportunity to succeed
	...feel responsibility for their part of the work
	...are treated equally regardless of their gender, race, ethnicity, faith, disability, sexual orientation or other characteristics not relevant to their role

VALUES GUIDES FOR CO-OPERATIVES	
CORE VALUES	VALUES IN ACTION. PEOPLE...
Equity	...feel that the way that decisions are made is fair
	...are treated equitably and with fairness
	...act in a manner that is impartial and non-discriminatory
	...are rewarded fairly for the work they do
Solidarity	...acknowledge and value different perspectives
	...value the participation of members of minority or disadvantaged social groups
	...pass on knowledge and learning to others
	...encourage trade with and support for other co-ops and like-minded organisations
Honesty	...speak up when it matters
	...act in a way that is consistent with what they say
	...are perceived to be honest and trustworthy in their interactions with others
	...Resolve tension or conflict through listening and dialogue
Openness	...Are inclusive, so that no one is left out
	...Value feedback, learning and development
	...Are able to access appropriate information
	...Value different approaches

VALUES GUIDES FOR CO-OPERATIVES	
CORE VALUES	VALUES IN ACTION. PEOPLE...
Social responsibility	...Support the organisation to contribute positively to society by working to address social or environmental problems
	...Encourage decision-making that takes into account the needs of future generations
	...Think through the impact of what they do on others
	...Are helpful in the communities in which they work
Caring for others	...Make a commitment to care for the natural environment
	...Treat each other with kindness
	...Appreciate the difference in others
	...Celebrate success

'Values are like bricks,' Marie Harder tells me. 'They need to be of the right size to fit together and to build on.'[38] This is the rationale for working with values guides – we can also call them principles, precepts or maxims – as they help to make it clear how you are expected to behave.

It is not a new model. In 1670, the Qing dynasty Chinese Emperor Kangxi issued the *Sacred Edict* 聖諭, consisting of 16 maxims, each seven characters long, to be published in every village in the country. One, at least, is relevant to businesses today – promptly and fully pay your taxes lest you need be pressed to pay them.

A participative health-check on values

Think of a red fox. Think of red lipstick on a leading actress such as Scarlett Johansson. The odds are that you are thinking of different hues of red. It is the same with values; we interpret them differently in different contexts. Single words can have multiple meanings, and single word values are open to multiple interpretations.

It helps therefore to give space for people to flesh out what the values mean to them. So, if you have a set of values already, then one exercise to explore them is to put them on cards, or post-its, and ask those participating to spend a few minutes ordering the cards, from high to low, with the following rounds – opening up to feedback and conversation after each round.

1. Which of these values mean the most to me, personally, and which less so?

2. Which of these values are we best at living up to, as an organisation, and which could we better at?

3. Which of these values are most important to us as an organisation going forward, and which less so?

As an exercise, you should allow for overlaps and for differences, but you have the opportunity, where there is consensus, to build on it, by:

- Asking for examples of options and actions in line with the priorities,

- Asking what team members can do to act in line with those values, and

- In time, exploring how to measure progress against those values.

You can do all of this if you prefer with a flipchart and stickers for people to score the values as a group. In my experience, though, the physical nature of cards helps to counteract the abstract tendencies of talking about values. After all, you can move seven values cards in over 5,000 ways.

You can encourage people to give illustrations of things that have happened in the organisation that chime with the values they are talking about, or that stop them happening. And if, through this, you are able to connect individual values with corporate values, that can be a light-bulb moment.

When we surveyed colleagues in my own organisation, asking whether they felt as if they were treated fairly – one of our core values – some were inspired, but overall we found that the results over time fell into two clear camps, with entirely different stories. When I ran discussion circles, mixing colleagues, to listen to what people understood by fairness, we saw that it meant very different things to different people. We had a job to do to be clearer on what the expectations should be, and how we could live up to that.

Bringing values to life

Either way, whether via a participative route, with a blank canvas or selecting from a longer framework such as the co-operative values, or via a professional route, the process of articulating, or reaffirming, values once formed is a critical point and core to whether they mean more than words on the page. It is relatively easy to make people feel good for a while, and for the values to go nowhere; the challenge is to do more.

This is a notoriously complex challenge, because to talk about values in the life of an organisation is like trying to tread on smoke. Everyone can see it is there, that it affects what happens, but it is not easy to capture and manage. As a result, it is common to develop value statements, and engage staff in a brief participatory exercise that soon fades away. It is harder to build values into the habits and life of the business; and yet this is where the real prize lies.

Values above all need to be tangible. Bringing the values to life is not just about internal communications within the organisation – another corporate video or CEO blog – but about translating values by putting them into context, in stores or offices or vans or on screens, and enabling dialogue to explore and build credible expectations of how people work and align with those values. Values can be 'primed' in this way. As Michael Sandel wrote in his book *What Money Can't Buy: The Moral*

values can create
ALIGNMENT

Limits of Markets, altruism, generosity, solidarity and civic spirit are 'like muscles that develop and grow stronger with exercise'.[39]

A well-developed set of values, coherent and shared across the business, has the potential to create a powerful alignment across the organisation, from top to bottom, side to side.

The environmental consultancy and charity Forum for the Future asks its staff team to vote on which value to prioritise for the period ahead. Staff champions help to be advocates and reminders of values in the workplace. Putting values into corporate communications, internally and externally, is a good reminder. Stories are powerful ways to transmit values. Engaging people emotionally is helpful, as values are often about instinct and feeling, more than logic and reason. Above all, you want to create enough of a common vocabulary and allow enough of a conversation across the organisation in relation to values.

The values fit

But the values that are championed still need to pass the 'values fit'. Do they flourish in the environment that the business is in? The story of Nokia is a lesson in what to do, and what not to do, on values.

In 2006, operating in 150 countries with 117,000 employees, Nokia decided to re-examine the values of the company. The company reached out to all its employees ('Nokians') through an online 'Nokia Jam', and to a smaller sample through a participative face-to-face process, the World Café, under the theme of 'a trip to the Moon'. Nokia held 16 World Café events around the world over the course of 60 days, each one attended by over 100 employees. Video blogs of the World Cafés logged around

30,000 visits, while 22,000 employees took part in an imaginative contest to choose photos to match the values, posting photos and voting online.

Four values emerged ('achieving together', 'engaging you', 'passion for innovation', 'very human') which were approved by a global meeting of 150 top leaders in the company. This was, in short, an exemplary process, but with one fatal caveat. In designing an open process and internal reflection across the silos of the organisation, Nokia sidestepped the two key cultural challenges the company in fact faced, which was competition between those silos and a lack of focus on the external environment.

In a fast-moving competitive environment, Nokia lost out as others made better phones cheaper. Olli-Pekka Kallasvuo, Nokia CEO from 2006–2010, now points to inappropriate values – internal competition and a lack of truth-telling – as a key factor in Nokia's subsequent failure. Silo politics, silo reporting and a culture of complacency spread naturally and quickly like weeds in a garden. In 2007, Nokia had half of the global market share for mobile phones. Today, it is an also-ran in the smartphone market, outpaced by its competitors.

Nokia chose new values, but failed to change the ones in place that were holding it back, which didn't match the reality that the business faced. Strategy professors Quy Huy and Timo Vuori conclude that

> **"just telling the truth could have saved Nokia's fortunes. Nokia's unfortunate decline again validates our affirmation that companies grew to greatness because they did something better than others. But they declined because they forgot to do common sense things ... to keep things from deteriorating, one needs to**

maintain a culture of honesty, humility, and co-operation inside the organisation. ❞ [40]

One of Nokia's values today, some years too late in a rapid and competitive technology marketplace and with one-twelfth of its former smartphone market share, is 'challenge: we are never complacent and perpetually question the status quo'.

It is sometimes said that strategy is 5% concept and 95% execution. The strategy professors extend this to suggest that execution is 5% technical and 95% people-related, where values, culture and emotion come to the fore. To get it right in good time, we now turn to the tools that can support work on values.

....

CHAPTER 7

Five Tools for Values

THE IDEAL IS TO EMBED VALUES in the life of a business, from top to bottom, in the same way that the beverage company Innocent was first to put its brand values over every inch of the drinks carton. If they are important, they can inform staff feedback, appraisal, competences, learning and development, recruitment and reward. Values can go beyond the workplace too, of course: supply chains and procurement, brand, customer service, product development and innovation. Ideally, values can be a source of business innovation.

In this chapter, we will look at five tools on how to implement values. To start with, here is a very simple game to get people talking about shared values.[41]

1. How to introduce values: a card game on co-operation

With a pack of cards and a pack of colleagues, divide people up into pairs and give every person two cards each, one red, one black. The value of the cards is unimportant. Each person is going to be asked to choose either the red card or the black card and to play it face down. There should be no speaking.

You can say that the purpose of the game is for those who are playing it to decide, but they will get scores once they have turned over their card. It can be helpful to write the scores up, so they can see them.

The rules are as follows. When the cards are revealed, the three possible combinations are scored like this:

LIFE IS LIKE... A GAME OF CARDS

Black card +3 | Black card +3
Red card +5 | Black card –2
Red card 0 | Red card 0

Give people ten seconds to choose which card to play, and then ask them to turn their cards over simultaneously.

If everyone keeps their score, then you can play this for a few rounds, to see if patterns of co-operation emerge. After each round, you can ask people why they played the cards they did – start off with the red–red combinations perhaps, then the red–black and then the black–black.

It can be fun. Some pairs are natural black card players from the start, some shift to black depending on what the person they are paired with plays, while others compete to get ahead by playing red. The discussion it prompts is where the value lies. Playing the red card is probably best for short-term profit, minimising risk for one player. But the black card probably delivers better returns over time, whether for one or both players. And is more likely, no doubt, to build values of trust, respect and integrity.

My degree was in philosophy, my professional life in economics. But, much as I have loved those, I wouldn't recommend them as a way in to talking about values. Better to let instinct, and play, kick in. As Jawaharlal Nehru is reputed to have said, 'life is like a game of cards. The hand you are dealt is determinism; the way you play it is free will.'

2. How to recruit for values

It is 9 am. Interview day. You have a long list of candidates due to come in and one of the key values you are looking for is ...empathy. What do you do?

Josh MacAlister has a model that works. His agency, Frontline, is one of the top 50 graduate recruitment agencies in the UK. His focus is to recruit graduates into children's social work.

'Empathy is notoriously difficult to assess people for,' he says. So what he has developed, as part of a wider assessment programme, is a ten-minute role play exercise, with a professional actor playing the role of a mum at school.[42] The role play is not about surprising candidates – they have been briefed that it is coming up. But empathy is not Gucci; it is not easy to fake. And using a professional actor (the alternative is anyone on the team who likes amateur dramatics) makes for a lifelike and consistent exercise across every candidate. The actor plays a distressed mum. She doesn't necessarily want to talk about risks that her child faces in her home life, but is willing to tell if the candidate builds a rapport. You know that the school has concerns already.

What doesn't work is a style of professional engagement that asserts authority, with an imaginary clipboard in front of you. The best candidates pause, attend to the mother in front of them, ask open questions, display interest. If they build a rapport, then the mother will be calmer and talk about risks that may affect their child. How then do you respond? A surprising number of people, says Josh, then swerve away from the tough conversation that needs to follow, whether it is drugs or domestic violence. They see it as too difficult. Some ignore it. The best find a way to take the conversation forward – 'tell me a bit more...'.

The role play is observed, and because self-reflection is one of the values they are looking for, alongside empathy, part of the assessment is also how people learn from the exercise.

A different role play I have seen, used by some medical schools in recruiting students, is one to test self-responsibility. Here are the instructions.

> *You work in the local bakery. At home, you have been having family problems that have made things very difficult for you. A month ago, you took an order for a gluten-free wedding cake. You forgot to put the order through to your boss when it was made. The wedding is tomorrow. It is now too late to solve or do anything about this. The mother of the bride is on the phone. She wants to know where the cake is. What do you say?*

If you try and bluff, or put them off, or put it down to your boss or your problems at home, that doesn't score well. The test is whether you can take responsibility, own up to it being your mistake, your fault ... and apologise.

Role plays are one possible tool. An alternative in interviews is to ask for personal examples of how people have operated, perhaps under stress, to explore their motivations and behaviours, and to use referees to test for values, such as honesty and integrity, not just performance and achievement. There are also psychometric tests such as from Hogan, typically designed for senior roles, which offer a profile of someone's values that can then be explored and tested in interview.

In health and social work, as with all of the caring professions, there are codes of ethics. These are designed to shape and sustain the quality and service of the role. The Hippocratic Oath for doctors is the great survivor, dating back, with changes over time, at least five centuries. Values are integral to a professional role that has power over life and death ...and patients probably wouldn't appreciate a motto over the doctors' clinic that said 'our values are to grow fast and make more money'. Even so, I sense that one reason it has endured is that, whereas many codes of ethics are rather abstract, rather apple pie, the Hippocratic Oath offers a clear set of values guides for how to behave.

'In our profession, people often refer to social work values,' says Josh, 'but they mean very different things to different people.'[43] He prefers to see values that can divide people, depending on their attitude. For social workers, for example, Josh suggests that a key value is whether you feel that people can change – that is a value statement that people can disagree with, so it is something you can start to use for selection. In recruitment for roles within the organisation itself, a core value is 'being brave' – something that gives a permission slip to those that want to take risks, but also helps to signal to those who don't that this is not the workplace that best fits them.

Using values to signal expectations is helpful to both recruiter and recruited. Forty per cent of executives fail in a new job, estimates

Stephen Harvard Davis, as they fail to understand the various cultures of the organisation they are coming in to. 'Knowing what makes different groups in an organisation tick is as important as being able to work with individuals.'[44]

3. How to build values in the supply chain

Cathryn Higgs, who is food buyer at the UK Co-op Group, says to me that 'values help me with my role. They give me the guardrail and help speed up decision-making. Understanding, living, breathing our values helps me make the right decision, particularly when I don't have time to consult.' For businesses with a global reach, training and support around personal integrity and business conduct has similarly been a key way to manage and mitigate risks when operating in markets with high levels of corruption.

When it comes to international supply chains, including those for global brand names from Nike to Primark, there is a good toolkit available for companies. There are a wide range of business and process standards, third-party assurance models, inspections, data and reporting to draw on, all depending on the nature and scale of the contract. However, the criticism is that far more effort in supply chains goes into auditing and certification of ethical values compliance than it does in terms of investment in those values directly.

When the eight-storey commercial building Rana Plaza collapsed in Dhaka, Bangladesh, in 2013 at a cost of over 1,100 lives, the failure was not simply one of inadequate certification from outside, but of inadequate voice for those inside. They knew the building they worked in – their values counted for nothing because they had no power and no voice in the decisions that ultimately took their lives. A values-based approach to supply chains, including a recognition of the enduring value of trade unions, would be more effective over time than today's armies of auditors.

Not surprisingly, perhaps, it is more common to invest in values where there is a long-term commercial interest. Retailers will care about their own-brand product ranges and their supply with more care than product lines that are on or off the shelf in short order. There is enough consumer interest in the provenance of food to keep them honest. Where you have vertical integration, such as from farms, then the values can be folded into different parts of the commercial chain. Where there are established suppliers, companies can do joint business planning.

As a result, there is, across the economy, increasing recognition of the value of long-term collaboration between businesses. Companies that are looking for long-term partnerships know how to develop joint ventures, knowledge pools or structured agreements that can build over time. PSA Peugeot Citroën and Toyota shared components for a new urban car, sold at the same time as the Peugeot 107, the Toyota Aygo, and the Citroën C1. Samsung and Sony, too, worked together to develop flat-screen LCD TVs. In each case, as in wider mergers and acquisitions, success was, in part, down to an understanding of the culture and values that were core to the participation of each company.

Kai Engel, Global Coordinator of A.T. Kearney's Innovation and Research and Development Practice, reports that 62% of businesses across Europe say that a quarter of business revenue is now due to collaboration around product and service innovation; 71% predict that, by 2030, co-operative innovation will account for over a quarter of their total revenues.[45] It is a good time to invest in the values of effective partnership.

4. **How to govern for values**

The default option for boards is to focus on what is easier to handle, which includes commercial outcomes, risks, financial profile and strategy. But values and culture are a responsibility of the board. As Jim Collins and Jerry Porras argue, 'companies that enjoy enduring success have core values and a core purpose that remain fixed while their business strategies and practices endlessly adapt to a changing world.'[46]

When I chaired the board of a global justice campaign, Jubilee 2000, which was advocating debt relief for the poorest countries in the world, values emerged time and again as an incentive for action and for results. Operational matters would dominate our agenda, but, whenever they looked as if they would take over, one of those around the board table would ask what it added to our core purpose, which was to cancel debts by the end of the year 2000. It was a powerful model of organisation, focused on a specific, tangible and time-limited goal. When we closed the campaign, having achieved extraordinary things, I made a comment that, all too often, people organising to do something can become people doing something for an organisation. A spirit of purpose and aligned values made us different, and gave us a restless desire to raise the game. In one country, Tanzania, the debt relief that was won by the campaign helped to eliminate elementary-level school fees and raise the school enrolment rate from 59% to 88% within three years.[47]

In governance terms, values should start in a practical way around the boardroom table. A code of conduct for board members now tends to be standard, and is a good place to include values guides on expected behaviours. Board members need the reflexivity to distinguish between their personal values and the shared values that are set for the business as a whole; but great boards avoid groupthink, and difference around how personal values should play out can be more creative than agreement, and far more so than avoidance.

The executive management should expect that a values test will be consistently applied to any recommendation that comes to the board. Alongside this, the framework of internal policies signed off by the board, from sound sourcing through to diversity and human resources, is one of the most practical tools on values that boards have. But remember the case of Barclays cited earlier, and the illusion of control. This is a tool to be used with care. Of course, policies set out what is and is not acceptable. But, implemented well, they should be a facilitator of shared values – like a conductor who helps to orchestrate musicians. How do people in the organisation already practise values that help? How can they be given the freedom to do that and more in their daily jobs? I have seen retailers that try to police the emotions of frontline staff – testing them for 'passion' on a Monday morning – but that is never a strategy for hearts and minds. It is better to start with asking people to be authentic, to be themselves and to be the best that they can.

The best policies are embedded in this vernacular of values and enabling, rather than being arbitrary or controlling. That is one reason that insight and understanding of organisational culture is an essential facet of board members' expertise. If the internal audit function reports to the audit committee, then that committee needs to be open to intelligence on culture, to soft data and examples of management behaviours that are out of sync with the business values.

In my work with the boards of the UK's co-operative sector, between them responsible for US$50 billion of turnover, I use a co-operative governance wheel, designed to set the performance and development of a board within the context of overall values and principles (see figure).

Linked to this is the accountability of the board to the ultimate owners, as it is they who set the formal rules and structure of the business. They may be the investors. In a co-operative, they are the members. In a co-operative, values and/or their associated principles are typically included in the articles of association, giving a mandate for action. There is a parallel here with B Corporation, the welcome and growing field of companies that write public benefit into the articles of the firm. There are moments like this in the life of every business, such as when a business founder retires and explores employee ownership as a way to take it forward, when ownership opens up and offers a way to lock in the values of the firm for good.

5. How to measure values

When it comes to values, how do you score honesty, fairness or courage? The answer is that there are three main ways in which you can: through people's perceptions, through indicative outcomes and through third-party assurance.

a. Perceptions

There are a range of proprietary workplace survey tools, such as the Organizational Culture Inventory. This is particularly useful for tracking how things are, compared to how things ought to be. The weakness is that it tends to be a one-trick pony. With the right facilitation and leadership, tools like this are very effective but, without, they are simply a more sophisticated, and more expensive, version of magazine self-help questionnaires – where the conclusions follow from the assumptions of the quiz setter.

The DIY alternative is to embed questions on values in existing surveys on a periodic basis. The Co-op Index, developed by Ryszard Stocki, Sonja Novkovic and colleagues, for example, is a multi-question survey on co-operative performance, designed originally for worker co-ops. On the ethical value of honesty, it tracks answers to:

- I trust people in our co-op.

- Members and employees are honest in their dealings with the co-op.

- Members and employees act according to strong ethical values.

- My co-workers find me reliable.

If you have agreed values guides, then measuring is more straightforward, as you can use the statements of behaviours as indicators of values in action. That may be through surveys, although in my experience the challenge is not asking questions of staff – that is now easier than ever – it is not asking too many questions of staff. You can also ask colleagues to observe and rate what they see. If a value guide is that 'people are inclusive so that no one is left out', how inclusive are staff meetings or an AGM in practice?

If you can benchmark the answers, that says more. If your values include being people-centred or customer-focused, then there are well-established survey benchmarks around things like employee engagement, workplace health and safety and 'net promoter' and other measures of customer satisfaction. In theory you can benchmark integrity, the most commonly cited business value. The Institute of Business Ethics runs surveys of employees in Europe and includes questions such as 'In your organisation's daily operations, would you say that honesty is practised...? Always / Frequently / Occasionally / Rarely / Never / Don't know.' In 2015 the lowest Always / Frequently response for a country was 63% and the highest 83%. Easy to compare you might think, but take care... to get an honest answer, staff need first to trust that they can be safe to say it how they see it: 100% 'always honest' may be the views of a cowed and fearful staff team.

b. Indicative outcomes

Anyway, surveys and observation tend to assess perceptions. They can't tell the whole story. Indirect measures, of outcomes that talk to the values that shaped them, are a robust way to cross-check what you find. For example, staff turnover rates, compared to sector averages, may give an indication of how fairly treated and managed staff are; gender pay comparisons and the proportion of women in senior and board roles are established measures of gender equality; while the ratio of highest-paid employee to lowest gives an indication of how equal an organisation is more widely.

c. Third-party assurance

Social indicators have taken off to the greatest extent in relation to equalities, driven by dramatic changes in societal values away from discrimination – along with an evolving legal framework in most countries which gives teeth to that value shift. In the field of equalities, businesses are blessed with third-party assurance systems that can tell us how we are doing. In relation to wider corporate social responsibility, again there is a wide range of tools for benchmarking and assurance, from triple bottom lines to an 'economy for the common good' balance sheet. This is not the book to list them: there are many such books in existence already, including others in the Dō Shorts series.

Even so, it is helpful to remember the limits to measurement. If you win awards, is that because you know how to win awards? If you run a regular survey on creativity, is that helping? If you measure trust, does that help build trust... or erode it? And we can recall Goodhart's Law which, adapted for this context, says 'if you set measures as targets, people will manage the business to hit that measure even if it means not doing the best for the business'.

So, how you measure your values should reflect those values. There are tools to use, but only if they prompt conversation and support good habits.

Values, like fairies, fade away if people don't talk about them, don't believe in them.

....

CHAPTER 8

The Values Checklist

I BELIEVE IN THE POWER AND POTENTIAL of bringing values back into commercial life. I say 'back', because business and markets always used to be understood in the context of a moral, usually spiritual, order. From Plato (whose ruling elite were not supposed to buy or sell property) to Aristotle (whose *Politics* commended the role of trade in preventing discord but regulated some of how it might happen), to the Christian Church fathers through to philosophers and theologians, such as Nicholas of Cusa, business was not an end in itself but part of a moral order directed towards the common good.

In a modern, secular and global context, business and markets are drawn with the black and grey pencils of exchange, finance and law, but they are still institutions, peopled and shaped by the colour of values underneath the surface – not just rational, but emotional, not just self-interested, but open to affinity and alignment. In business terms, these are also resources. Values can help you to uncover the hidden potential of your business.

But there is also an urgency to the values agenda. The 'wild facts' of climate change, resource constraints and species loss are collective action problems, as are the trends towards wider social inequalities. For a sustainable future, these are challenges that require a response from leaders, of business as much as any other sector, that is rooted in values.

As powerful as self-interest can be, only ethical values can encourage people to go beyond their own or their group interests and understand themselves as a collective. This isn't just about encouraging ethical businesses, but about ensuring values-based markets and economies. Values can help us to come together.

So, while there is no one right set of values, there is power and potential in making the most of the shared values that are right for the business you are in. It takes time to build good practice when it is under way – and extraordinary efforts to change when poor practice is entrenched. A cookie-cutter approach to values – select some, throw them up – will work if you want something to display on your corporate website, but it will offer little more than that. To bring values to life, for the genuine transformative potential that they offer, values will be an implicit, and occasionally explicit, part of the rhythms and dance of commercial life.

The following checklist is intended to be a resource, as a prompt for possible actions, rather than a list of requirements. What measures do you do? What measures could you take?

Articulating values

- Does the organisation have an agreed statement of shared values?

- Are these values published and available?

- Are the values translated into expectations around everyday behaviour?

Leadership on values

- Is the strategy and direction of the organisation informed by its values?

- Do those with responsibility lead by example?

Governance on values

- Does the board consider values and track performance and risk in relation to them?

- Does the board consider external assurance and stakeholder feedback in relation to the values of the organisation?

- Are values integrated in the framework of policies approved by the board for the business?

The values fit

- Are the values in line with the core purpose or founding story of the organisation?

- Are the values the right ones, in terms of their fit with the wider market and society within which the organisation operates?

Ownership and awareness of values

- Do those involved in the business know what the values are?

- Do those in the business believe that the values are ones that they care about?

- Do the values inform the conversations, communication and planning of those within the business?

Integration of values

- Are values integrated in human resource management – such as performance review, learning and development and colleague recruitment and induction?

- Are values integrated into commercial relationships – such as buying decisions, supply chain management, and partnerships?

- Are values integrated into marketing – such as communication, product and service design and innovation?

Accountability on values

- Do values form part of the accountability framework of the business to its ultimate owners, for example in dialogue or in the articles of association?

- Do values form any part of what the business reports on or discloses externally?

- Are the interests and perspectives of stakeholders considered in the way that values are handled?

APPENDIX

Key Definitions

Values are standards of behaviour – a judgement about what is important in life.

Shared values are the motivations, explicit or implicit, that can be considered to be part of the culture(s) of an organisation.

Ethical values are values that make a broader, normative claim about the right way to live or act.

Principles are precepts based on values that are intended to direct behaviour.

Values guides are statements of how people may behave in context in line with specific values or principles.

Co-operative and ethical values are values developed for use in the co-operative sector and set down in a global Statement of Co-operative Identity.

The **values–action gap** is the difference between what people do on ethical values compared to what they say they would like to do.

The **values fit** is the extent to which shared values have resonance in the wider context that an organisation operates in.

Notes and References

1. *Oxford English Dictionary*. 1933 edition.

2. Greene, J. (2014). *Moral Tribes: Emotion, Reason, and the Gap Between Us and Them*. New York: Penguin.

3. Wilson, J. (1997). *The Moral Sense*. New York: Free Press.

4. Cited in Sennett, R. (2012). *Together: The Rituals, Pleasures and Politics of Cooperation*. New York: Allen Lane.

5. O'Toole, F. (2015, December 15). Obscene salaries encourage contempt for the simple dignity of a job well done. *Irish Times*. Retrieved from http://www.irishtimes.com/opinion/fintan-o-toole-obscene-salaries-encourage-contempt-for-the-simple-dignity-of-a-job-well-done-1.2449165

6. Harder, M. *et al*. (2015). *Starting from Values*. University of Brighton. Retrieved from https://www.brighton.ac.uk/_pdf/research/lhps-groups/starting-from-values-legacies-booklet-web.pdf

7. Salz, A. (2013). *Salz Review: An Independent Review of Barclays' Business Practices*. London: Salz Review.

8. Brinded, L. (2015, July 8). The fired Barclays CEO had two nicknames inside the bank that tell you why he was forced out. *Business Insider*. Retrieved from http://uk.businessinsider.com/barclays-ceo-antony-jenkins-left-because-of-his-lack-of-investment-banking-understanding-2015-7

9. Odell, M. (2015, May 20). Trader transcripts: 'If you ain't cheating, you ain't trying'. *Financial Times*. Retrieved from https://next.ft.com/content/eac637ae-fefb-11e4-84b2-00144feabdc0

10. Sparknow (2013). *The Salz Review's Seventh Element*, Sparknow. Retrieved from http://www.sparknow.net/publications/salz_review_seventh_element.pdf

11. Harding, R. (2013). *The Collaborative Entrepreneur*, Think Piece 8. Manchester: Co-operatives UK.

12. Lencioni, P. (2002, July). Make your values mean something. *Harvard Business Review*.

13. Great Place to Work (2015). *Organisational Values.* London: Great Place to Work Institute UK.

14. Crompton, T. (2016). Personal correspondence.

15. The text that follows, with some changes, has been published in an earlier form as Mayo, E. (2016, March 4). The business case for values. Retrieved from **https://edmayo.wordpress.com/2016/03/04/the-business-case-for-values/**

16. Great Place to Work (2015). *Organisational Values.* London: Great Place to Work Institute UK.

17. *Ibid.*

18. Oxford Economics (2014, February). *The Cost of Brain Drain: Understanding the Financial Impact of Staff Turnover.* Oxford: Oxford Economics.

19. Lampel, J., Bhalla, A., Chordia, M., & Jha, P. (2014). *Does Employee Ownership Confer Long-Term Resilience?* London: Cass Business School.

20. Pérotin, V. (2016). *What do we really know about worker co-operatives?* Manchester: Co-operatives UK.

21. Labaton Sucharow (2012). *Financial services professionals feel unethical behavior may be a necessary evil and have knowledge of workplace misconduct.* New York: Labaton Sucharow LLP.

22. Cannell, B. (2015). Personal correspondence.

23. Co-operatives UK (2016). *The Co-operative Option.* Manchester: Co-operatives UK.

24. Co-operatives UK (2015). *The Co-operative Economy.* Manchester: Co-operatives UK.

25. MacPherson, I. (1996). *Co-operative Principles for the 21st Century.* Geneva: International Co-operative Alliance.

26. *Ibid.*

27. Eid, M., & Martínez-Carrasco Pleite, F. (2014). *The International Year of Cooperatives and the 2020 Vision*, Euricse Working Papers, 71.

28. The text that follows, with some changes, has been published in an earlier form as Mayo, E. (2014, March 9). Co-operatives and executive pay. Retrieved from **https://edmayo.wordpress.com/2014/03/09/co-operatives-and-executive-pay/**

29. Wheeler, D. (2016). Personal correspondence.

30. Harrison, R. (2013). Presentation at Ethical Consumer/New Internationalist 'People Over Capital' Conference, London, 27 September 2013.

31. Talent Futures (n.d.). *Values Exercise.* Retrieved from **http://www.talentfutures.com/articles/Values%20Exercise.pdf**

32. Fredén, J. (2015, September 24). *Ingvar Kamprad, Founder of IKEA.* Sweden.se. Retrieved from **https://sweden.se/business/ingvar-kamprad-founder-of-ikea/**

33. See Grayson, D. (2004). *The Value of Values.* Auckland: RentonJames.

34. George, B., & Sims, P. (2007). *True North: Discover your Authentic Leadership.* San Francisco: Jossey-Bass.

35. *Ibid.*

36. Strohminger, N. (2016, January 30) cited in *New Scientist* (2016, January 30). The essential you. Retrieved from **https://www.newscientist.com/article/2075030-who-do-you-think-you-are-4-rules-can-help-you-know-yourself/**

37. This list draws on and adapts indicators selected from: Coop Index, a project that was developed in Canada from 2007 for worker co-operatives, **http://coopindex.coop;** and We Value List of Indicators (2013 update), Sustainable Development Coordination Unit (SDeCU) at the University of Brighton, **http://blogs.brighton.ac.uk/wevalue/the-research/.**

38. Harder, M. (2016). Personal correspondence.

39. Sandel, M. (2013). *What Money Can't Buy: The Moral Limits of Markets.* New York: Penguin.

40. Huy, Q., & Vuori, T. (2014, March 13). What could have saved Nokia, and what can another companies learn? *INSEAD Knowledge*. Retrieved from **http://knowledge.insead. edu/strategy/what-could-have-saved-nokia-and-what-can-other-companies-learn-3220**

41. I learned this from Dave Dulson, who worked with BP on values change, following the Deepwater Horizon oil spill.

42. MacAlister, J. (2016). Personal correspondence.

43. *Ibid.*

44. Davis, S.H. (2005, May). 40% of Executives in a new job fail. *Organisations & People: The Journal of AMED*, 12(2).

45. Mayo, E. (2015). The case for economic co-operation. *Huffington Post*. Retrieved from **http://www.huffingtonpost.co.uk/ed-mayo/the-case-for-economic-coo_ b_7702264.html**

46. Collins, J., & Porras, J. (1996, September/October). Building your company's vision. *Harvard Business Review*.

47. President's Office, United Republic of Tanzania (2004). Letter, 17 February 2004.

....